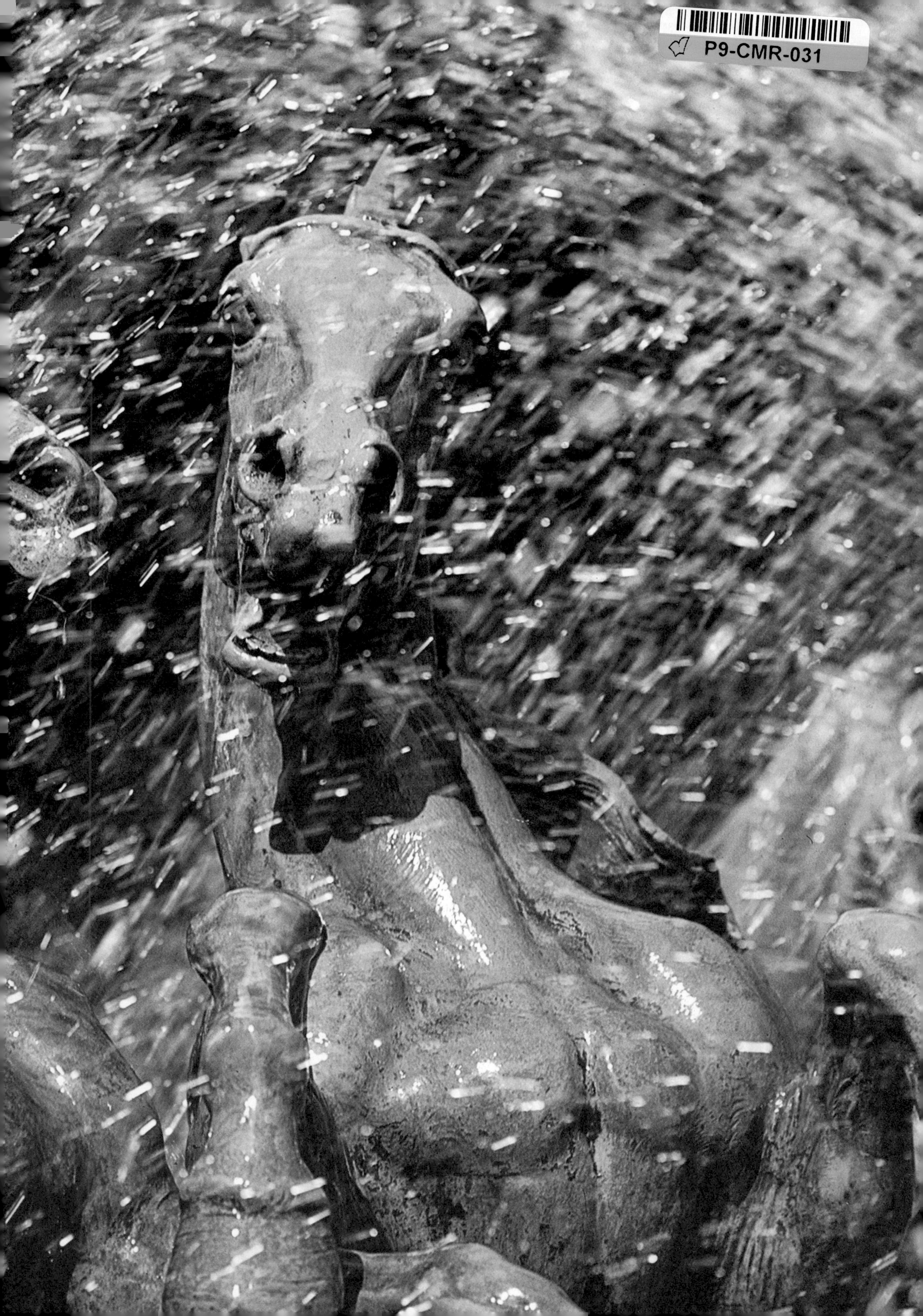

PARIS

Designed and Produced by

Ted Smart & David Gibbon

COLOUR LIBRARY INTERNATIONAL

Introduction

PARIS is a city that celebrates the successful marriage of reason and romance with an enthusiasm that keeps it forever young. Its symbol and most popular souvenir is the Eiffel Tower. Wherever you go in Paris there is the Eiffel Tower; it sticks out like a King Kong of Meccanoland above the mansart roofs; it is found on ashtrays, musical boxes, as decoration for gateaux and even in little plaster globes which when shaken cover it in a blizzard.

Could there be a more romantic concept than that of a tower, built entirely of cast iron in the middle of a city? The notion is almost as extravagant as putting rubber tires on the Paris Metro or erecting a museum of modern art that looks like an oil refinery. Both such startling innovations of recent years have had a mixed reception from the outspoken Parisians.

Speaking their minds is a characteristic of Parisians but to speak it clearly and logically is as important as the content of the message. This tradition goes back to the twelfth century when Peter Abelard set the world of education on its ear by suggesting to his ecclesiastical masters that knowledge comes from life experience interpreted by logical thinking. This doctrine, at a time when most thought was conditioned by scholastic Church dogma, was put forward by Abelard at Notre Dame, the great Church that dominates the Île de la Cité.

The Île has lost many of its medieval buildings since those days owing to the rebuilding fervor of Napoleon III, but there is still the old palace, now the Law Courts, with the strikingly elegant Sainte Chapelle and the Conciergerie which was the antechamber to the guillotine at the time of the Revolution.

During this period, reason was taken to an absurd and tragic extreme, and in the more lucid light of our own times nothing seems more absurd than that the revolutionaries should have renamed the Cathedral of Nôtre Dame the Temple of Reason

At the downstream end of the island there is a wooded point which by contrast could be called the Temple of Love. Its real name is not inappropriate for it is known as the Vert Galant, a nickname for Henry IV, a very sensible king who not only brought the religious wars in France to an end but had a proper appreciation for the beauty of Parisian women. Fifty three of them became the mistresses of this 'gallant evergreen'.

A romantic spot with its green trees, the vert galant, is a charming place to sit and enjoy the view of the Seine with the Louvre on the right bank and the Pont des Arts crossing to the Institut de France on the other, if, that is, you can find room among the young couples who gather in the shadow of King Henry's equestrian statue which discreetly turns its back to them.

Young people abound in this part of Paris. The Latin Quarter is just across King Henry's Pont Neuf Bridge, actually the oldest in Paris despite its name. Here are the University of the Sorbonne and the Beaux Arts School as well as other ateliers and educational establishments. Along the narrow streets are art galleries, bookshops, restaurants, cafés, and all with an individuality that reflects their owners' character. The main arteries of the quarter are the Boulevard St Michel, known as the Boul 'Mich', and the Boulevard St Germain. Along the Boul 'Mich' there is all the vitality of student life. In summer the cafés spread out across the pavements under the plane trees and the waiters speed about with trays of lager, bottles of wine, giant French loaf sandwiches and plates of sausages and 'frites'. In winter the tables crowd into the glass-covered greenhouses that allow the Parisians to enjoy pavement café life even in January.

The fame of the Latin Quarter and of St Germain des Près where Jean Paul Sartre launched the philosophy of existentialism which underlines modern attitudes has made it an area for the tourist safaris that set off every morning from the Place de la Madeleine and other tourist bases. The double decker panoramic buses with their perspex sides browse for a while at the Place de St Germain des Près with its old medieval church, stop at the Luxembourg Palace which Henry IV's wife Marie de Medici turned, nostalgically, into an Italian-style Palazzo and return to their bases on the right bank.

Paris is used to tourists and goes out of its way to put on its best attire and make-up for them. It oozes romantic nostalgia like some expensive perfume by Lanvin. Most of all it does this in the quarters between the Opera and the Arc de Triomphe. Here are wide boulevards, the splendid squares, the solid, ornate buildings of the incredibly romantic Imperial dream that swept Europe in the nineteenth century from the

The setting sun hangs low and diffuses its glow over the splendor of Paris left.

old Hapsburg Empire to the Atlantic. It is surprising that this display of imperial grandeur and rich bourgeois ostentation should have followed so closely in the steps of a revolution that was to bring equality, fraternity and freedom to all. It is even more so that in our present-day democratic world we should all be so bewitched by a world that was so patently based on inequality and privilege.

Or is it? Napoleon, who was fairly perceptive about people, knew that pomp and pageantry appeal to mankind and as soon as he became secure as the chief of the French he began to put up splendid monuments. The Madeleine was intended as a Greek Temple dedicated to his soldiers, and for the sake of symmetry he changed the façade of the old Bourbon Palace across the Seine into a Greek Temple too. He also ordered the building of the Arc de Triomphe, though it was only finished in time for his body to pass under it on its return from St Helena years after the ex-Emperor's death.

After the Eiffel Tower, this splendid triumphal arch at what used to be called the Etoile, but is now called Place General de Gaulle, is the most important Paris landmark. It evokes Napoleon's short-lived Empire and is bigger than any of the triumphal arches put up by the Romans. It also looks down on an avenue which is unique. The Champs Elysées is the grandest avenue in the world, and the most romantically named. In Greek times, Elysium was a state of ideal happiness and the abode of the blessed after they had shuffled off this mortal coil. There is nothing dead about the Champs Elysées, however. The traffic speeds up and down, the cafés are packed all hours of the day and night, the cinema billboards spell out their messages of sex, romance and adventure, the airline offices open sheer windows onto exotic worlds, Fouquet's elegant restaurant stares across the boulevards at an international hamburger chain and the most expensive cars in the world reflect the boulevard lights.

You don't actually have to do anything in the Champs Elysées except sit. It is a great production worthy of Busby Berkely and all you have to do is be the audience. That is what most of the people sitting in it are: a world audience waiting for the show to begin. The funny thing about the Champs Elysées is that nothing does happen except on special occasions when it becomes the stage for military parades or demonstrations of national grief, joy or discontent.

Scene setting for big productions is something the designers of Paris all had in common. Gabrielle, who designed the Place de la Concorde at the start of the Champs Elysées, could hardly have imagined the kind of spectacle that would fill his great square however. At the Tuileries end, the guillotine was erected and front row seats, for the execution of the King and Marie Antoinette and the leaders of the revolution, were occupied by those busy 'tricoteuses', the name given to the old women who were forever knitting as the heads rolled.

If one knows about it, the spot before the Tuileries gates where the heads fell to Monsieur the Razor gives one a slight chill up the spine. The worst kind of madmen are the reasonable ones and in this case they themselves became victims before the nightmare came to an end. But a glance through the Tuileries gates brings the nasty day dream to a rapid end as one sees the children playing round the fountain with their mothers or nurses making sure that Gaston or Jean Paul do not fall in. There are some charming paintings of the Tuileries by the Impressionists whose museum is in the Jeu de Paume by the Rue de Rivoli corner of the gardens. They show people sitting on those rather uncomfortable metal chairs drinking coffee or beer and watching children on the merry go round. The scene is not all that different today, the Tuileries gardens are a very mothers-and-children kind of place even though the statues do depict ladies in various states of undress more likely to appeal to the boulevardier than to Mamam.

Where the Tuileries Mamams come from it is difficult to say because north of the gardens is the smartest quarter of Paris, full of jewelry shops, dress shops, perfume shops and discreet notices which tell you that the goods on sale are not for the general public but only for people of the highest rank or very rich.

Most people do not do their shopping here but go to the architect Haussman's Grands Boulevards which in the nineteenth century were the places for a stroll and for picking up girls in a very roundabout and discreet way, and today are the popular shopping streets.

Parisian department stores are like a gigantic trunk that won't close properly. All the contents spill out on the pavements into stalls which sell so many products that you wonder what can possibly be left inside the shops. There are people demonstrating potato-peeling machines, liquids to remove stains from leather, clockwork toys, shoe repair outfits, folding baby carriages and innumerable other gadgets. Passers-by, and there are always plenty of them, can't help stopping to look and while they do so they probably remember that although they don't want an electric hair curler they do need a new nightdress so they go into the Aladdin's Cave.

There is something overwhelming about big stores and though Parisians like them for some things, when it comes to food there is nothing like the neighborhood épicerie, run by Madame assisted by her children or her husband. These, like the bakeries with their tantalizing smell of fresh bread floating out into the street, are the truffles in the Paris paté. Anyone who has any doubts about the French sensibility to cuisine needs only to walk into an épicerie to have them quelled. The pots on the marble shelves sound like a gastronomic poem; Paté de campagne, Paté de fois avec truffes de Perigord, Tête de veau, Andouilettes, Tripe a la mode de Caen, Saucisson d'Arles, Choucroute Alsacienne and what a splendid variety of cheeses; Camembert, Pont Aven, Brie, Rocquefort, Port Salut, Bresse bleu, each one as distinctive as the area they come from.

Though the great markets at Les Halles have moved out of the center of Paris and left only a rearguard of restaurants in their wake there are still plenty of small markets left in the arrondissements. Here the French housewife goes about the business of buying food with the care and attention that it merits.

Markets are cheaper than shops, or should be, and the food is fresher, or so it is believed. They are also more romantic. The rows of stalls, piled with great green artichokes, golden peaches, live crabs and lobsters, unplucked chickens, and caged rabbits attract visitors as much as the Parisians themselves. Paris is well endowed with markets; there are flower markets on the Île de la Cité and, at the week-end, a bird market, there are wine markets and fish markets, book markets and furniture markets and the greatest show market of them all at Porte de Clignancourt, the Flea market.

Everyone goes to the flea market, which extends over a large area and sells everything from cigar butts to antiques. Some go out of curiosity, others are professional buyers. You can see them talking to the stall owners over a coffee in a corner of the shop. Some go for the bargains and a great many go in the hope of making some remarkable discovery: an unknown Delacroix, an unpublished letter of Madame de Sevigny. Most romantic of all is the thought that the market is the receptacle of millions of peoples' lives expressed in their possessions. Who could possibly have owned that chest of drawers encrusted with bits of glass or the wooden leg with a mother of pearl

boot? The Marche aux Puces, to give it its French name, is a window into other peoples lives much as into Paris itself.

In Paris there are plenty of vignettes of the city's life; the fishermen who sit patiently along the banks of the Seine, the flame swallowers who entertain the crowds outside the Georges Pompidou Museum, the filles de joie at the Bois de Boulogne with their bold stares, the smart ladies at the Café de la Paix with their miniature dogs, the passengers crowded on the rear platforms of single decker buses, the smart blue-uniformed policemen urging the traffic to keep moving, and the endless works of art.

These are the images of Paris, the movie flashes that remain in the memory, but there are also the clues picked up by the other senses. The sounds of Parisian songs half sung, half spoken, defiant, world weary, nostalgic and sentimental. Their greatest singer was Edith Piaf. The piping cheeky notes of the accordion, the rapid staccato of an announcer's voice on Radio Paris, the smell of good cooking wafting down a narrow street, of gauloise in a café, the scent of expensive perfume in the Rue du Faubourg St-Honoré, the damp autumn atmosphere of the evening hour that Parisians call L'Heure Bleu. The feel of the bark on plane tree trunks, of cool water in the Tuileries fountains, the taste of oysters and chablis, of hot onion soup, and of the glasses of Pernod or Dubonnet over which one can linger at some café table, absorbing their flavor and that of the Parisian scene of which they are an essential part.

Most of all, Paris leaves one with the impression of a city in which there is a logical mind at work. Henry IV, Napoleon, Louis Phillippe and Napoleon III all employed talented architects and planners to change the face of the city, so that today we have the Paris that stretches from the Place des Vosges through the Place de la Republique, the Grands Boulevards, the Place de la Concorde, the Champs Elysées and onwards to the Bois de Boulogne to enjoy.

The Paris of the future is already taking shape at the new skyscraper quarter of La Défense and in the midst of artistic Montparnasse. Fast city motor routes dive along the banks of the Seine, and the Museé Georges Pompidou sets the style for a new concept in art galleries and cultural centres.

The scale and enthusiasm of these projects is romantically inspired, their execution logical. What the ultimate value of them is, the Parisian public will decide. In the meantime they provide travellers with a contrast in time with the Paris of their love affair.

Car lights blaze beneath the majesty of the Arc de Triomphe overleaf.

The intricate wrought ironwork of the Eiffel Tower soars 984 feet into a pale blue sky left. Constructed for the Centennial Exposition of 1889, commemorating the French Revolution, the tower was conceived by Alexander Eiffel, an eminent bridge engineer, and literally constructed in a matter of months.

The elegant turn-of-the-century Alexandre III bridge can be seen right against the deepening blue of a twilight sky, its pretty lamps shining high above the gently flowing Seine. At the four corners of the bridge are set the columns that are adorned with graceful, winged statues, one of which is shown below.

From the bridge an excellent view of Les Invalides may be seen above, with the dome of the Hôtel des Invalides silhouetted against the night sky.

The familiar vista of the Eiffel Tower above is sharply contrasted with the unusual view left as floodlighting illuminates the ironwork of the tower, leaving darkened crevices where the lights cannot reach.

The majestic Opéra is shown right amid a blaze of lights, while below and overleaf the Conciergerie, on the Île de la Cité, is reflected in the still, dark waters of the Seine.

The tree-lined avenue of the Champs Elysées, with its pavement cafés *above, below* and *below left, leads* from the Arc de Triomphe to the Place de la Concorde, and it is hard to imagine that it was originally designed as a military road.
Situated on this fashionable avenue is the Renault Building in which can be seen *left* the exciting prismatic reflections.

Leafy green trees frame the art nouveau entrance to the Metro on the Rue des Abbesses *right, while* overleaf *in the Jardin des Plantes,* the dense foliage in the tree-lined pathway offers a cool haven where visitors can sit or stroll.

In the heart of historical Paris stands the avant-garde edifice of the Georges Pompidou Center above and below left, a cultural and artistic complex dedicated to the furtherance of modern arts and offering both permanent and special exhibitions in which the visitor can actively take part.

The replica of New York's mammoth Statue of Liberty above, standing on Port de Grenelle, symbolises the amity of Franco-American relations and in the background can be seen the modern structure of the Radio France Building.

Contemporary Paris, in common with many cities, has her share of towering skyscrapers, below and right, while overleaf, her most famous landmark, the Eiffel Tower, stands aloof in a pink-washed sky.

Old Paris

IN a city with the rich history of Paris the past often sinks out of sight under the weight of the centuries but the frugal nature of the French has, except for one or two moments of frenzied iconoclasm, allowed certain areas of old Paris to remain untouched, crumbling away through the process of age rather than at the demolition squads' sledge hammers.

The oldest quarters lie north and south of the Île de la Cité. Here, monks built monasteries inside the massive wall, with 67 Towers and 6 doors, still visible at the Rue des Jardins St Paul, and erected by King Philippe Augustus from the Louvre where he built a fort to beyond the Ile St Louis.

On the Left Bank of the river is the St Severin quarter, where winding, narrow streets still evoke the atmosphere of the Paris of Héloïse and Abelard. After his quarrel with the monks at Nôtre Dame, many teachers and students deserted the island and moved to the Left Bank to follow his teachings. They grouped themselves around the church of St Julien-Le-Pauvre and St Severin, where the galleries around a medieval charnel house look much as they would have done to Abelard.

Street names reveal the character of the neighborhood; there is the Parcheminerie where letter writers and scribes lived and the Rue de l'Ecole de Médecin in which the surgeons practised every kind of operation without the benefit of anaesthesia. In the Rue des Anglais congregated English students who, like other Europeans, had made the journey on foot or horseback to learn from the French teachers whose fame was spreading far and wide.

Today, these streets are full of ethnic restaurants – Chinese, Arab, Indian – and cellars where traditional Parisian and French songs help revive the atmosphere of old Paris.

This quarter was the starting point of the pilgrimages to Santiago de Compostela in Spain, one of the great religious centers of the Middle Ages, and churches and monasteries provided pilgrims with food and shelter before their long journey. The Hôtel de Cluny, built on the ruin of Roman baths, became an important headquarters where Mary Stuart was once among the famous guests.

Many of the pilgrims must have walked down the Rue de Mouffetard which, with its old houses and signboards and the market stalls that crowd it in the mornings, still has the air of medieval days when traders shouted their wares in the streets and people of all nationalities gathered there en route to Spain.

To the north, across the Ile St Louis, lies another area of streets and crumbling houses that the visitor rarely sees. This is the Marais, the center of fashionable Paris at the time of Henry II, who was killed while jousting in the Rue St Antoine, and of Henry IV who built the Royal Square, now known as the Place des Vosges. Henry, whose success with the ladies may have had something to do with his Queen Marie de Medici's refusal to live near him in the Royal Square, wanted to turn the Marais quarter into the most brilliant in Paris. The Place Royale was the center of fashionable life, pageants, and parades; and even duels took place there. Only the nobility occupied the houses that today look rather sad and neglected above the arcades where Richelieu and Madame de Sevigny once lived.

The history of Paris during this period and until the Belle Époque is well documented at the Hôtel Carnavalet nearby in the Rue de Sevigne. Many of the rooms from houses in the neighborhood have been transferred complete to the museum and paint more vividly than words can describe the lives of their former occupants. The Maráis was deserted by fashionable Paris after the Revolution and today its streets have a decaying charm in which the ghosts of those who frequented them would appear perfectly at home. Many of the houses are now being renovated and this worthwhile exercise may save for posterity an important period of Parisian history.

A mania for rebuilding is what destroyed much of the atmosphere of the real centre of old Paris, the Île de la Cité, but Nôtre Dame and the Sainte Chapelle still stimulate images of medieval Paris in the mind.

The newly cleaned stonework of the great cathedral once again shows it as it looked when Mary Stuart was crowned Queen of France on her marriage to Francis II, and is one of the most magnificent in Christendom. Its architecture and the countless stone carvings that decorate its front, its towers and spires, is the work of thousands of masons, sculptors, carpenters and iron workers whose combined but individual work comes together in a glorious expression of the medieval spirit.

Inside, the solid pillars that support the roof rise to the galleries and stained-glass windows through which the light pours. Standing in this vast shrine to an enduring faith in God and Paris, the spectator is carried back to the great events that took place under the 115 feet high roof. Phillipe Augustus brought the Crown of Thorns from Venice here; Henry VI of England became King of France at the altar; Henry IV of France, before his conversion to Catholicism, married his bride from the entrance steps since he was not allowed to enter; Napoleon crowned himself Emperor and Josephine Empress; and after World War II, the leaders of the free countries of the world congregated here to celebrate victory and affirm their faith in the freedom of mankind.

In contrast with Nôtre Dame, which expresses the solemnity of man's commitment to himself and his fellow men, the Sainte Chapelle is a symbol of life's joys. The slender, elegant building seems all light and colour with windows supported by pillars and buttresses that appear too fragile to have remained so well preserved for seven hundred years.

It is the spirit and wit of Paris materialized just as Nôtre Dame is the expression of the indomitable character of the capital of France and cultural center of the world.

Parisian night-life is renowned the world over and offers a variety of entertainment. Neon lights blaze and beckon the merry-maker; to the Folies Pigalle far left; the Moulin Rouge above right, reminiscent of the days when Toulouse-Lautrec would record on canvas the artistes of his era; and, of course, the restaurants and brasseries, above, near left and right, where food and wine are to be lingered over and enjoyed at leisure. Eating alfresco is particularly popular in Paris, and as dusk falls and the mellow lights cast long shadows, the guests can sit idly over a glass of wine, enjoying the coolness of the evening breeze.

One of the city's major attractions is the famous Folies-Bergère Theater where sumptuous and colorful displays, illustrated on these pages, can take months of careful planning.

At the opening of the new theater, in 1869, the Folies presented a varied programme which included Paul Legrand as Pierrot, and although forced to close during the siege of Paris in 1870, when it became a political meeting-hall, on its re-opening the theater became once more a bustling arena.

Édouard Marchand was responsible for the introduction of girls to the Folies and when, in 1894, striptease became the vogue of the music halls, the theater seized the opportunity of elaborating the theme and became renowned for its provocative displays of female nudity. The large, lavishly equipped stage, with its extensive range of lighting equipment, provides many magnificent settings for the theater's extravaganzas.

By night Paris glows, with a wealth of entertainment available, ranging from opera to the exotic. The brightly lit streets above and above right, *with their suggestive signs* right *are an integral part of city life.*

Yet amid the harsh glow of neon signs, the soft raindrops glisten in the darkened streets and the deserted pavement café left *lends a momentary air of melancholy.*

Cars passing late at night overleaf *leave nothing but the glowing trails of their rear lights, amidst the myriad illuminated signs, as an indication of their presence.*

The equestrian statue of Henri IV page 35 *was erected in 1818 to replace an earlier one destroyed during the French Revolution. Built of bronze, the statue commemorates 'Le Vert-Galant', France's most popular king, who, although a Huguenot, converted to Catholicism to take the crown, for, he declared, "Paris is worth a Mass".*

Down with the monarchy

ON July 14 Paris is in a gala mood. The little squares and streets of each arrondissement are full of tricolor bunting. Flags fly from masts and on the balconies of houses, there is a special mass said in the Church of Nôtre Dame, dancing in the streets, and nobody goes to work. It is the anniversary of the day in 1789 when the Paris crowd marched on the Bastille prison and released its seven prisoners.

Only a column now rises in the space where the prison once stood, for it was quickly demolished after its fall. A contractor named Palloy made souvenirs of the stones, locks, hinges and other details and sent them all over France to announce the news of the great moment of freedom.

But the fall of the Bastille did not cure France's ills. There was a shortage of food, and rumors that the monarch was celebrating at Versailles, so the people marched there to bring him back to Paris where he became a prisoner at the Tuileries, a palace later burned down during another crisis of internal strife. Meanwhile law and order was breaking down, vandals were destroying some of the treasures accummulated by the monarchs of France, and people who had represented authority were being killed and their heads displayed on pikes. A commune was formed at the Hôtel de Ville and Danton incited a gang of thugs to massacre priests at the Carmelite Church. A feast of the Goddess of Reason, with dancers from the Opéra, was celebrated at Nôtre Dame.

Next the mobs began to destroy royal statues including those of Henry IV on the Pont Neuf and Louis XIV in the Place Vendôme.

A section of the Convention government, known as the Mountain, wanted to kill Louis XVI too, but others, the Girondins, wanted to spare him. In the midst of this turmoil Charlotte Corday, an admirer of the Girondins, found her way into the revolutionary Marat's house in Rue de Hautefeuille on the Left Bank and stabbed him to death in his bath.

The guillotine, invented by a Dr. Guillotine, as a 'philanthropic decapitating machine for sheep', was installed, first at what is now the Place de la Nation and then at the Place de la Concorde.

The King of France was kept prisoner at the Temple, later razed in order to prevent it becoming a shrine, and he made his last journey from here to the Place de la Nation, then called Place du Trône.

Queen Marie Antoinette's last view of Paris began at the Conciergerie on the Île de la Cité. Her trial had taken place there and she had been condemned to die. She was thirty-eight, and on her last ride through the crowds, some jeering but others silent with the revulsion that was soon to be turned on the revolutionaries themselves, she behaved with the dignity of a queen.

The monarchy was dead and now the quarrels between the new leaders of the nation increased while the people starved. Herbert, Danton and Desmoulins were themselves caught in their own web. Nearly 1,400 heads rolled under the guillotine in six weeks during the Reign of Terror and finally its main author Robespiere himself was arrested and beheaded at the Place de la Concorde.

There followed enormous rejoicing at the thought that the terrors of the Revolution were over; dancing broke out in the streets, and in the dance halls that sprang up the new German dance, the waltz, was introduced. The boulevards were crowded and fashionable clothes were no longer an invitation to be arrested.

But the troubles were not over yet and riots and revolution continued. Now the public made fun of their politicians and longed for an all-powerful sovereign to lead them back to normality. When he arrived in the guise of a young Corsican lieutenant, they rallied to him with a loyalty and energy that overran Europe and destroyed the foundations of the monarchical system.

In modern Paris the Revolution is just a scene from the play called the History of Paris. Even the number of people killed no longer has the same significance in a century when the motor car is more lethal than the guillotine and wars number their victims in millions. Nevertheless, like most extremes of violence, the Revolution has left its ghosts to haunt the places where the violence took place, and has left also the happier evidence of people whose dedication to the preservation of the things of value saved the culture of France for posterity.

Among these are the Louvre which, thanks to the efforts of some members of the Assembly, became the storehouse of the works of art of the aristocratic houses that were being looted and vandalised. The Convent of the Petits Augustins became the famous Beaux Arts of Paris at which so many of the world's painters and sculptors have studied.

'A bas la monarchie', cried the Revolutionary crowds, but they voted for two Emperors and another king before settling for the Republic they have today.

The Maison of Christian Dior, with its elegant couture, sumptuous furs below and expensive perfumes left, epitomizes the fashion-consciousness of Paris.

Twice a year buyers gather from all over the world to watch sleek models glide gracefully down the catwalk above, right and overleaf and interpret, for the prêt-à-porter market, the exquisite clothes which only the wealthy can afford to buy.

Dior's sensational 'New Look', introduced in 1947, with the backing of Marcel Boussac, a textile manufacturer, became a phenomenal success and it was largely due to Dior's subsequent widely acclaimed collections that Paris was re-established as the supreme fashion center.

One of the most famous and busiest department stores in Paris, *Au Printemps*, *these pages and overleaf left houses a superb collection of merchandise where the discerning shopper can purchase a coveted item bearing the prestigious Parisian label that is synonymous with wealth and luxury.*

Shopping in such a store as Au Printemps, even though crowded, is always a pleasure for the sales staff are both courteous and helpful and , if required, are only too willing to gift-wrap each article with care and expertise.
The pretty glass window above right *makes a pleasant diversion from the sea of goods on sale, and* overleaf right *the rooftop restaurant, under its magnificent domed ceiling, provides a place to rest and take refreshment during the shopping spree.*

The attractive displays in the shop windows are a very real indication of the quality and range to be found inside this Aladdin's Cave. Every taste is catered for, from the perfume hall right, *with its incredible range of alluring fragrances, to the huge toy department, a veritable wonderland for wide-eyed, small shoppers. Elegant clothes in profusion, made as only the French know how, with meticulous attention to cut and cloth, prove a great temptation to over-spend.*

44

The Louvre Museum *left and far left, housed in a section of the Louvre Palace, is one of the world's richest treasuries of art and antiquities.*

The unequalled painting collection represents all periods and includes the superb canvas above *by Jacques-Louis David, portraying the Coronation of Napoleon and Josephine.*

In addition to the outstanding accumulation of paintings, the museum has an extensive collection of Greek and Roman, Oriental and Egyptian antiquities, including sculpture and exquisite objets d'art. Furniture of the 17th and 18th centuries is beautifully displayed in the Cour Carée, and there are also special national museums reserved for the art of Africa, the Far East and the South Sea islands.

The sumptuous interior of the Georges V Hotel, *illustrated* above right, center right *and* right *is representative of the high standard to be found in Parisian first-class hotels, and offers the discriminating guest exquisite décor and excellent service.*

Napoleon lived here

NAPOLEON Bonaparte's military successes did not blind him to the fact that fame is ephemeral and that in the long run men are remembered by the creative works they have left behind. He therefore set out to remodel Paris and to encourage a Napoleonic culture which would forever be identified with his period.

Thanks to this ambition, the world has been able to add the Napoleonic style to its history of furniture, costume and art, and Paris possesses buildings and bridges which might otherwise never have been erected.

The first signs of a preoccupation with posterity and perhaps his first intimations of mortality appeared after Napoleon's return from his Egyptian campaign when the French navy had been sunk by Nelson's ships at the battle of Aboukir Bay.

Faced with political setbacks at home, Napoleon, back from Egypt, set about persuading the Parisians of the glories of the campaign there. Around the Place du Caire, the streets were given Egyptian names and Egyptian motifs appeared on the buildings. In the Rue de Sèvres, on the Left Bank, a fountain featured an Egyptian farmer, and Prince Eugene de Beauharnais, son of Napoleon's wife Josephine, decorated an entire house in the Egyptian style.

Napoleon's real work in improving Paris did not begin until he had become First Consul, after surviving an attempt on his life. As Consul he found himself master of France and of its finances. He employed the architects Percier and Fontaine and set about making a city that the future would remember him by.

First, he completed the Cour Carré of the Louvre and began to fill the palace with the spoils of his successful campaigns. After defeating the Austrians in Italy he brought back Roman statues and Renaissance paintings and even the famous bronze horses from St Mark's Basilica, though the latter were later returned.

After Austerlitz, he built one of the most charming triumphal arches in the world at the Carousel between the Louvre and the Tuileries and opened up the Rue de Rivoli. Today, with its arcaded shops and shuttered houses, it is one of the prettiest shopping streets in Paris.

In addition, though these works are not normally visible to the visitor, Napoleon improved the sewers and drains and the city's water supply. To the average Parisian, the battles, the roar of the cannons, the smoke-filled valleys through which the cavalry charged, the cries of the wounded and dying, were as distant as an adventure story. What were real were the results of military successes. They reminded the people of Paris where their new-found wealth came from. Two bridges built across the Seine at this time bore the names of important battles: Pont d'Austerlitz and Pont d'Iena. Streets and squares were also renamed after battles and generals.

In the Place Vendôme, a column made from two hundred and fifty cannons captured at Austerlitz was erected and a statue of Napoleon dressed as a Roman Emperor placed at the top. This was later replaced, first by a statue of Henry IV and then by a fleur-de-lys, but the Third Republic brought back the original which surveys Paris today from its perch one hundred and forty three feet above the Place.

In his efforts to change the world and provide a style of living different from that of the old world monarchies, Napoleon adopted the ideas of the ancient Greeks and Romans. In them he, and those who supported the ideal of France reborn, saw the virtues that made nations great: simplicity, purity, dedication, patriotism and faith. Nôtre Dame was reconsecrated and Napoleon was made Emperor; by placing the crown upon his own head he made the point that it was he who ruled and not the Church. He ordered a Greek-style temple in honor of his soldiers to be built at the top of the Rue Royale which leads up from the Place de la Concorde, and today the Church of the Madeleine is one of the most important of the Parisian landmarks.

The virtues of the noble Romans was celebrated in paintings by David who also painted Napoleon at his coronation and on other splendid occasions, such as the distribution of the eagles to his regiments.

The monuments of Napoleon's Paris still remain as a testament to one of history's more remarkable and intriguing personalities, a man who was coldly ambitious yet romantic, ruthless yet generous, a man who could say 'No dying soldier ever cursed me, no man was ever more loyally served by his troops,' and believe it.

In France the memory of the Emperor lives on, and nowhere more than in Les Invalides. Here are the uniforms, arms and flags of the Grande Armée and the Emperor's grey overcoat and simple furniture brought back from St Helena. In the Dôme Church is the body of the Emperor himself, set in a circular crypt surrounded by statues representing each of his campaigns from the Italian to Waterloo. Near him lies the body of the King of Rome, the small son on whom his hopes of founding a dynasty had rested.

Standing majestically on the hill of Montmartre the white domed basilica of the Sacré Cœur right looks out over Paris.

The colorful quarter of Montmartre overleaf, situated on the right bank of the Seine, has long been the favorite haunt of artists, and in the Place du Tertre center right painters exhibit their works in the time-honored tradition. Pavement cafés below, bistros left and above right, bakers below right, often with attractively decorated façades like the one shown above, help preserve the Bohemian image.

It is many years, however, since the real Bohemians vacated Montmartre as it became a fashionable tourist attraction, nevertheless the flavour remains, to be savoured by the many thousands of visitors for whom Paris would not be Paris without wandering round this still beautiful village.

49

The streets of Montmartre are filled with artists young and old painting for pleasure, or in the hope that their canvasses might prove irresistible to the tourists who daily throng the busy by-ways.

Dominating the skyline is the unmistakable dome of the Sacré-Cœur, seen overleaf left in the view over Montmartre and overleaf right from the Place du Tertre.

Bonjour Monsieur Haussman

IN 1846 the population of Paris was just over a million; twenty years later it was nearly two million, and the city had had a face-lift that made it the most elegant, sophisticated, fun-loving city in the world. This happened during the period of the Second Empire when Paris, under the rule of Napoleon, was carried away by the champagne dream of a revival of the glories of the first Napoleon.

The man most responsible for the rebuilding was Georges Haussmann, whom Louis Napoleon appointed Prefecture of the Seine. Monsieur Haussmann came from Alsace; he was an energetic man with big ideas and the backing to carry them out. He intended to convert Paris from a city of overcrowded houses, narrow streets, few water mains and streets illuminated by lanterns, into a city of wide boulevards and splendid mansions lit by 32,000 gas lights. The Ville Lumière, as its visitors later called it, not just for the lights alone, but for the gaiety and brightness of its spirit, was being created.

One of Haussmann's first moves was to open avenues along the old gallo Roman roads that crossed the city. From north to south across the Île de la Cité, and from Gare de L'Est to Denfert Rocher then called the Place d'Enfer–the Square of Hell he opened the Boulevards now called de Strasbourg, Sebastopol and St Michel. From East to West, he lengthened the Rue de Rivoli and made the Grand Boulevards that run from the Place de la Republique to the Madeleine. At the Arc de Triomphe he planned twelve new roads radiating outwards; the place, now called Place Generale de Gaulle, was then more appropriately named Etoile – the Star. He built the Opera Square which immediately became the center of fashionable Paris. From here, along the Boulevards des Capucines, les Italiens and Montmartre, the smart crowds of the second half of the nineteenth centry gathered and promenaded.

The men, in fashionable English-style moustaches and daringly smoking in public, complemented the ladies who followed elegant fashions set by the Empress Eugénie, whose flair for dress is still renowned.

Today, the liveliness is still there, but it is more democratic. American-style drug stores have replaced the smart cafés and souvenir shops have taken the place of the smart milliners and shoe shops. Instead of the crinoline there are jeans, and cars instead of landaus clutter the streets, in which fashionable people once paraded their wealth and social station.

At the Café de la Paix by the Opéra there is still an atmosphere of times gone by in the carved wall panels, the mirrors and the faded pastel colours of the decor. And the Opéra Comique, further along the Boulevard, still stands though it is now known as the Opéra Studio, and is used as a training school for the singers and musicians of the Opéra instead of producing the delightful operettas of Lehar and Offenbach.

Though the scene has changed, Haussmann's spirit still remains in the solid grey mansions with their balconies and decorations of stone flowers and fruit. His name is preserved in the Boulevard Montmartre and where the great department stores spill their contents on to stalls on the pavements.

Not all Haussmann's ideas were as inspired as those of the Boulevards, however, and to many Parisians the destruction of the heart of the city on the Île de la Cité is still a subject of regret. Here, where once the royal palaces had stood amid old medieval houses which crowded to the very doors of Nôtre Dame, Haussmann opened a great space and erected a solid block of buildings to house all the administrative and legal services of the city of Paris. The medieval island which was the setting for Victor Hugo's famous Hunchback of Nôtre Dame ceased to exist except in a few corners found today alongside the Cathedral itself.

Louis Napoleon also had his own ideas on how to make Paris the most beautiful city in the world. He added to the Louvre Palace the great buildings surrounding the main courtyard, with their elaborate mansard roofs and towers and he ordered the creation of a huge park, modelled on Hyde Park in London, at the Bois de Boulogne, formerly a royal hunting forest. Two lakes were dug, where today Parisians row themselves and their children about under overhanging trees, and pavilions and restaurants were erected. The Bois became the Parisian playground where people could picnic on the grass, ride on the bridle paths or attend the race meetings at Auteuil and Longchamps.

Within the grounds of the Bois is a charming garden and house known as the Bagatelle, which was owned by the Hereford family and the contents of which formed the basis of the Wallace Collection in London.

In its new setting, Paris bubbled and sparked its way through the Belle Époque to the sound of champagne corks, the Can-can and the Polka. The enormous confidence which buoyed it up and gave it the spirited life which attracted visitors from all over the world received a sudden shock when Napoleon declared war on Germany in 1870 and was defeated in six weeks. The city's natural vitality brought about a quick recovery, however, and in 1878 Paris celebrated its revival with a Universal Exhibition on the slopes of Chaillot above the Seine. A few years later, another exhibition saw the building of the most famous of all Parisian landmarks: the Eiffel Tower.

Haussmann, now a Baron, saw it completed before he died. Perhaps he felt it was the fitting crown to all the work that he himself had accomplished during his life in remodelling Paris into the city that plays host to many millions of visitors every year.

Paris abounds in statuary and monuments and throughout the city can be seen many splendid examples.

'Le Triomphe' above *is one of the decorative relief-sculptures on the Arc de Triomphe commemorating Napoleon's military victories and is the work of Jean-Pierre Cortot. At the base of the monument lies the Tomb of the Unknown Soldier* below, *lovingly decorated with wreaths.*

The magnificent statue of the Grand Palais below right *depicts Victory, her chariot drawn by four sturdy chargers, while in the tranquil gardens of the Jardin des Plantes* above right *is the monument to the noted naturalist, Georges-Louis Leclerc, Comte de Buffon.*

As night falls and the roar of the traffic diminishes, the imposing façade of the Petit Palais center right *is bathed in a golden glow of light.*

Amid the bustle of city life can be found many quiet areas where it is possible to relax and reflect, or engage in solitary pursuits; especially rewarding during the late afternoon when sunlight filters through the dense green trees, and the solid roar of the traffic seems far away.

For some, however, the comradeship of perhaps a card game, or a gambling game played for higher stakes is a more enjoyable way of passing the time.

The deserted café overleaf appears strangely forlorn in its amber glow, but when the new day breaks the crowds will return and bring color and clamor to enliven the scene.

58

The beautiful Gothic cathedral of Nôtre-Dame, below, below left and overleaf *is situated on the Île de la Cité and its magnificent buttresses and spires are particularly awe-inspiring when viewed from one of the bateaux-mouches* right *which daily tour the ancient island, the heart of the city.*

Inside the cathedral, with its three exquisite rose windows, still retaining their original 13th century glass above, *supplicants can augment the profusion of flickering candles* left *with a prayer of their own.*

Artists and writers

THE melting pot of the post revolutionary ideas that swept through Europe in the nineteenth century was a community of artists and writers that gathered in Paris along the slopes of the hill of Montmartre.

Here a colony of creative men and women who would change the forms of established means of artistic expression lived and exchanged ideas at cafés like the Guerbois, Aristi de Bruant's Chat Noir and the Lapin Agile on top of the Butte de Montmartre, and worked in the old houses that lined the streets at the foot of the hill. The opening of the Moulin Rouge in 1889 provided them with another place of entertainment and gave Henri Toulouse-Lautrec a theme for his life's work. He was an aristocrat whom an accident had crippled and he immortalised the famous music hall by painting the entertainers: La Goulou, Jane Avril and a snake hipped dancer whose supple movements earned him the name of Valentin le Desosse.

Other artists who frequented the quarter were Degas, the elegant dandy who immortalised the ballet dancers of the Opéra and the horses of the racecourse in the Bois de Boulogne, and, earlier, Manet, whose painting of two silk-hatted gentlemen picnicking with naked ladies in the park shocked Paris.

Though many of the painters lived in Paris their inspiration was drawn from nature – or so they thought. In fact, the Impressionists, as they were disdainfully called, were basing their ideas on a theory whose seed bed was the logical and intellectual concepts which were a product of the intellectual life of Paris. Science was all the vogue, and what could be more scientific than the explanation of vision as the impact of particles of light reflected from objects onto the retina of the eye. The Impressionists, led by Monet, set out to produce those insubstantial flecked paintings, whose logical end was the painting of Seurat, the pointillist painter of the well-known Paris river scene at the Island of Le Grande Jatte.

Resisted at first, the Impressionists became the darlings of collectors; particularly Renoir, the most sought after of them all with his paintings of glowing, buxom girls who fitted so satisfyingly into the tastes of the men of the Belle Époque.

Though the painters were working towards depicting those agreeable aspects of nature which the new bourgeoisie could enjoy (and still can at the splendid collection in the Jeu de Paume) the writers of the period reflected a more somber scene. Liberal ways of thought freed them to explore subjects hitherto not suitable for written work. Their precursor was Balzac who, like Dickens, explored every aspect of life to the full. The Parisian author, whose house at Rue Raynouard contains his furniture and relics, had such an appetite for it that he was continually in debt. Zola, who followed him, an indefatigable worker, like his friend Cezanne in painting, produced books that set out the lives of people who had never been considered worthy sub-

jects of the novel. In Nana, he followed the career of a slum girl who became a demi-mondaine of the type found on Baron Haussman's Grand Boulevards; in Germinal he traced the story of a family of miners.

Other writers, like Maupassant and Proust lived the agreeable and self-indulgent life of men of the Belle Époque and at the same time examined it with critical objectivity. Maupassant succumbed to the good life, passing his last years in an asylum, the victim of syphilis, and Proust turned his back on it, becoming a recluse in his cork-covered bedroom at 102 Boulevard Haussman. The new-found freedom to live and explore life to the full was summed up in the title Balzac gave to a series of his books, The Human Comedy, but as time went on, much of the early gaiety of Montmartre became tragedy.

The honor roll of those who opened up the avenues to modern art often sounds like a roll call of disaster: Modigliani, suicide; Pascin, suicide; Van Gogh, suicide; Utrillo, the superb recorder of the Montmartre scene, death from drink and drugs; Toulouse Lautrec, death from drink.

By 1914 Montmartre had ceased to be a genuine center of the arts and had become the bohemian Disneyland of tourists. Night clubs with fanciful names like Heaven, staffed by angels, and Hell where you were served by devils, multiplied like mushrooms. The filles de joie paraded up and down the streets and promised all kinds of exotic entertainments, whilst the Place du Tertre was filled with hack painters waiting to paint portraits. The artists and writers had left and gone to Montparnasse across the river.

Here Picasso tore reality into pieces and reassembled it to his own design. From copying the world of God, artists now tried to be the Creator modelling life in the shape of their own subjectivity. Braque followed suit, Matisse scribbled his glorious arabesques, Chagall gave rein to his Russian visions. The creative vitality of Paris was unimpaired and now thousands of students from overseas arrived, thirsty for a drink at the source in the studios of La Grande Chaumière, at Colarossis, at Julians, and the Beaux Arts.

They came hoping to catch a glimpse of, or at least to breathe the same air as, the giants of modern art, but by then they, too, had dispersed just as the previous generation of painters had done from Montmartre. This time the artists went south to Provence to carry on their productive and separate lives.

Today the world of Montparnasse heads towards another future; a fifty-six story tower rises where the old Montparnasse railway station stood and other modern buildings are going up all round. They are the tangible evidence that the new ideas launched over fifty years ago are now accepted by all, that the new world envisaged by the pioneers of modern art has actually arrived.

Paris is a gourmets' paradise and provides an excellent variety of establishments, from sleek restaurants previous page, to informal cafés and bistros these pages in which to sample her world famous cuisine.

Wine is an important accompaniment to any meal and France's renowned vineyards can supply the best, whether it is a humble vin du table, or a particularly fine château-bottled vintage.

France is justly celebrated for her many culinary
dishes, always beautifully and temptingly
displayed. Most restaurants, from the ritzier
establishments above to the humbler cafés
overleaf, offer a varied menu which usually
includes a special 'plat du jour' and a wide range of
delectable desserts.

Freshly baked bread right is an essential part of
the French way of life and the prolific boulangeries
provide a delicious assortment, including their
typical long loaves, crusty rolls and croissants.

The Seine

THE river that flows through Paris from east to west suddenly, as if reluctant to leave the city, curves back upon itself at its western end and flows east again before returning to its route towards the sea. Between the Seine and Paris there has been a long love affair since the first Parisians installed themselves on the Île de la Cité and held it against barbarians and Normans.

Until the last hundred years few bridges linked the two banks and the river has not been hemmed in by warehouses and other buildings to reduce it to a mere canal in an urban environment. In return for this consideration, the Seine has brought into Paris the flavor of the countryside of France and on its smooth and plentiful waters it has borne the barges laden with the produce of French farms and vineyards.

At its entry into the capital from the south the barges unload their crates of wine from Burgundy, Bordeaux and Champagne, at the Halle aux Vins. Further along the quaysides, there are piles of timber from the Vosges, building stone, steel beams, and crates of manufactured products from all France. Here is the port of Paris, and the Seine is the carrier of supplies to keep the city going.

If you follow the course of the river downstream under the Pont d'Austerlitz, built to commemorate Napoleon's greatest victory, you soon have the green trees of the Jardin des Plantes (Botanical Gardens) in view on the left bank. Built in the time of Louis XIV for the cultivation of herbs, the gardens later acquired a zoo, created during the Revolution, with animals taken from the menageries at Versailles.

Within sight is the Île St Louis, one of the most attractive corners of Paris, with its seventeenth-century buildings. In the narrow and tranquil streets there are massive doors studded with nails, well-proportioned façades in the classical style and a peaceful air not found in the busy boulevards. Gautier, Baudelaire, Wagner and the painter Sickert all lived here at one time or another and the island is still the sought-after haven of artists and writers whose talents enable them to pay the rents of this idyllic spot.

The Ile St Louis is like the dinghy of the great galleon that is the Île de la Cité, with the great bulk of Nôtre Dame filling the sky. The river divides to go round it, the northern arm sliding under the Pont St Louis, and the other passing reverently under the Archbishop's bridge and between the high concrete walls which guide its passage past the cathedral.

At the far end of the Île de la Cité, by the triangular prow of the Vert Galant, the two arms of the Seine greet each other again. The grotesque faces of the carvings on the Pont Neuf look on with medieval mirth at the meeting which seems like a symbol of the human encounters that take place under the trees.

The quaysides of the Seine begin at this point; broad restful terraces where men can sit for hours bent over a fishing rod catching nothing, or reading. Couples watch the play of light on the water that flows on under the Pont des Arts, the Seine's simplest bridge made of iron and wood by Napoleon's orders, and leading from the old Louvre to the Institut de France.

The racing traffic along the fast routes by the river no longer allow lingering strolls under the plane trees with the Louvre stretching like an endless architectural frieze, but in the quiet mornings or late at night something of the old magic can be recaptured.

Opposite the Tuileries, there are some large barge-like vessels moored by the quaysides which puzzle those who do not know their use. They are the floating swimming pools of Paris where on hot summer days one can sit around a pool of pure, filtered water enclosed by the walls of bathing huts that surround the pool and admire the chic bikini'd beauty of Parisian ladies.

This is the most frequented part of the river bank and from the Pont de la Concorde, built partly with the stones of the Bastille, there is a view that takes in many of the major landmarks of Paris. To the north, on the hill of Montmartre, the Basilica of the Sacré Coeur stands out; much nearer, across the square and up the Rue Royale, the Madeleine Church is framed by the buildings of the Hôtel Crillon and the Hôtel de la Marine. To the left is the entrance to the Champs Elysées with the splendid Marly horses on their columns, and on the Left Bank rises the Palais Bourbon and National Assembly.

Now the river passes under a splendid iron bridge with solid iron lamp standards and wreaths of iron leaves; this is the Pont Alexander III, erected at the time of the 1900 Paris exhibition in homage to the Czar. From this bridge the Avenue du Maréchal Gallien leads straight to Les Invalides and Napoleon's last resting place.

At the Pont de l'Alma, built to commemorate a battle in the Crimean War, are moored the broad glass-topped boats known by the charming name of bateaux mouches after their inventor M. Mouche. On them one can take a trip up river and back while dining in the restaurant aboard.

A less grand kind of pleasure boat, which rubs shoulders with the huge and sleek barges which bring produce to Paris, is the vedette. These leave from the Pont Neuf and the Iena bridge, which celebrates Napoleon's victory against the Prussians. Here the Seine flows in the shadow of the Eiffel Tower whose huge iron grid soars into the sky.

To Jean Cocteau, the writer, poet and film director of the intellectual Paris of the twentieth century, the tower is as significant to Paris as Nôtre Dame. It also marks the exit of the river from historic Paris, though not from its future, for as it loops round the Bois de Boulogne and nostalgically turns for a last look, it passes the new quarter of La Défense, where granite and steel and glass buildings rise like a miniature Manhattan on the direct line of boulevards which run through Paris from the Louvre through the Place de la Concorde, the Champ Elysées and the Arc de Triomphe.

Erected in memory of those who died during the 1830 and 1848 revolts, the July Column right, in the Place de la Bastille, stands 169 feet high.

The magnificent panorama on page 77 encompasses the broad sweep of the Invalides Esplanade, from the Pont Alexandre III, to the high dome of the Hôtel, under which lies the body of Napoleon.

Within Paris the plentiful parks and gardens provide cool, green oases where visitors can rest from the busy round of sightseeing and where residents may linger over the daily news or enjoy a game of boules.

Paris has many beautiful gardens, including the lovely Jardin du Luxembourg with its delightful Médici fountain; the impressive Jardin des Plantes which contains the oldest tree in Paris as well as over 10,000 plant species, and the Jardin Fleuriste de la ville de Paris, where are grown the flowers which will eventually be planted in the city.

French patés and cheeses are among the finest in the world and even the smallest épiceries, such as the ones shown center right and on page 84 are sure to stock a large assortment, including brie, camembert, roquefort and neufchâtel.

The discriminating Parisians, in common with their fellow countrymen, take full advantage of the delicacies on sale, from the wide range of cooked meats, with savouries such as smoked ham and sausages, seen amid the overwhelming display overleaf, to the plentiful array of fresh meat on the boucher's slab above.

Exotic side-salads, delicious mayonnaise and specially prepared mushrooms tempt the shoppers, page 85, while above right the carefully arranged fruit and vegetables in the foreground of the grocer's shop are, typically, of the highest quality.

The extensive range of mouthwatering pastries proves a bewildering choice for the ardent shopper right, and the colorful blooms of the flower stall left perfume the air with their delicate bouquets.

The food markets of Paris, and there are almost eighty of them, including the famous street markets on Rue Mouffetard, La Rue Lepic and La Rue de Buci, provide first-class quality fruit and vegetables from which the Parisian housewife can carefully choose.

The meticulously arranged displays, piled high with juicy grapes, luscious peaches, bright red tomatoes and a wide variety of vegetables such as aubergines, peppers and fresh green beans, attract the many shoppers, ever anxious to secure a 'bon marché' or good buy.

The Art of cooking

IN Paris, the food of love is what is cooked in long, slim-handled frying pans or braised in earthenware casseroles and music does not enter into it except in restaurants catering for tourists. Usually, the French eat their meals accompanied by a hubbub of lively chatter, for food is part of social life, the fuel that stimulates the imagination and helps to release conversation that can be as piquant or bland as the sauces that accompany the dishes.

Caring about food begins in the market place and Paris is well provided with places where the housewife can find a veritable cornucopia of the products of France: artichokes from Provence, grapes from Languedoc, chickens from Bresse, lamb from Brittany, oysters from La Rochelle, lobsters from Roscoff and red mullet from the Mediterranean.

According to tradition, it was the wife of Henry II, Catherine de Medici, who brought about the change from robust cooking to cuisine in France by bringing chefs from the Medici court when she arrived from Italy. Perhaps what prompted her to do so was the enormous banquet consisting of 30 peacocks, 33 pheasants, 21 swans, 9 cranes and an equally large number of other birds as well as goats and pigs with which she had been regaled on a previous Italian visit.

Whether it was her influence or not, French eating habits changed radically in the sixteenth century. Instead of the one knife and pewter goblet seen in early sixteenth-century prints, table settings began to include forks and long-handled spoons as well as other cutlery and linen table sets. The tableware included Venetian glass, Faience and Nevers porcelain.

By the time of Louis XIV many other refinements had been introduced and there were experts who gave advice on dishes fit for the Kings and Queens of France.

It was not until the nineteenth century that the public restaurant arrived on the scene. The reason for this was the Revolution which, by destroying the aristocratic families, put their cooks out of work and obliged them to start cooking for a wider public.

One of the oldest restaurants in Paris, and one of the most expensive, is the Grand Vefours behind the Palais Royal. After the Revolution this became a place frequented by Napoleon and Josephine, whose names are engraved on a brass plate behind their favourite seats. Another is Laperouse on the Île de la Cité. This old mansion of the Counts of Brouillevert still retains its atmosphere of faded tapestries and low ceilinged rooms. Maxims' is a world-famous restaurant reminding everyone of the Belle Époque and Franz Lehar's Merry Widow.

Most restaurants in Paris – and there are over eight thousand of them – do not have such a distinguished lineage but are small bistros where frequently the patron and his wife do the cooking and serving, or which are run by a chef or head waiter who has learned the art of good catering at one of the grander or more famous of the world's hotels or restaurants.

Each arrondissement has its own restaurants, and their atmosphere is often coloured by the local environment. In the Opéra, Palais Royal and Champs Elysées area, fashionable and expensive restaurants abound but so do the cheap, self-service cafeterias which cater for the tourist.

The Latin Quarter also has its fashionable restaurants but, because of the vast number of students from every part of the world who study there, it also possesses a vast international range of eating places.

In the little streets off the Boul'Mich there are literally hundreds of the bistro type of restaurant, often with paper table covers and menus written in almost illegible handwriting.

Towards the Montparnasse area the restaurants frequented by the avant garde artists and writers of the twenties are plentiful. At the corner of the Boulevard Montparnasse and within sight of the Luxembourg Palace is the Closerie de Lilas, one of the most popular places to dance and pick up ladies in the nineteenth century, and a favorite haunt of Ernest Hemingway in the twentieth. Near the Boulevard Raspail smart café restaurants make from tourists the profits that were lean when their patrons were impecunious artists and writers.

And at St Germain des Près the name of Sartre and Simone de Beauvoir still pack in the visitors to whom Existentialism sums up a way of life of the post war years.

Across the other side of Paris, up on the hill of Montmartre, there are more restaurants of the tourist kind exploiting their association with the days when Montmartre was the home of Impressionist and Post Impressionists, while down below on the roads that lead to the Place Clichy and Place Pigalle the show goes on at the Moulin Rouge and the Crazy Horse Saloon, whose juxta-position in this quarter introduces a note of surrealism which sums up the strange transfiguration of this area of Paris.

Despite the millions of tourists who arrive each year to take over the restaurants and cafes in Paris, there are always those which resist being taken over. In them, food remains the main thing and even if the tablecloth is made of oil cloth and the menu illegible and the toilet dirty this is often a sign that everything is being given its right priority.

Silhouetted against the soft glow of the setting sun the statue above is situated in the vicinity of the Arc de Triomphe du Carrousel.

The mime artists above right and the fire-eater below create a colorful diversion outside the Georges Pompidou Center.

Scattered along the city boulevards are the newspaper stands below with their wide range of journals and inevitable display of souvenir postcards.

Built in the 17th century, the grandiose Palace of Versailles *above left, with colorful blooms dominating the south parterre* above and overleaf, *was created by the flamboyant Sun King, Louis XIV, whose statue* below *is sited in the impressive courtyard.*

The beautiful and extensive gardens contain superb statuary, such as that illustrated right *and the delightful boating lake* left.

91

The splendor of the Palace at Versailles, with its sumptuous furnishings, and now one of France's richest museums, is matched by the beauty of its magnificent gardens.

Le Nôtre's imaginative concept transformed the landscape surrounding the Palace into peaceful gardens, wooded areas, lakes and terraces, where the King and Queen could escape from the rigors of court life and rest amid the tranquil greenery; and here were built the Grand and Petit Trianons.

One of the features of the Petit Trianon is the picturesque Queen's House above and above right where Marie Antoinette played the role of tenant farmer in the romanticized setting of a poor village hamlet.

The many visitors who now throng these beautiful gardens can feed the fish right or sail their model boats left, but when the last of the tourists have departed the gardens become, once more, the peaceful haven so beloved by kings and queens of ages past.

Except for one solitary figure, night falls over Paris, and the deserted gardens in the vicinity of the Arc de Triomphe du Carrousel are bathed in the soft glow of the setting sun, overleaf.

95

First published in Great Britain 1979 by Colour Library International Ltd.
© Illustrations: Colour Library International Ltd.
Colour separations by La Cromolito, Milan, Italy.
Display and text filmsetting by Focus Photoset, London, England.
Printed and bound by Rieusset, Barcelona, Spain.
ISBN 0 906558 01 8
COLOUR LIBRARY INTERNATIONAL